Where Is He?

by Carlos Santiano

NATIONAL GEOGRAPHIC ▪▪▪ **Hampton-Brown**

National Geographic and the Yellow Border are registered trademarks of the National Geographic Society.

National Geographic School Publishing
Hampton-Brown
www.NGSP.com

Printed in the USA.
Quad Graphics, Leominster, MA

ISBN: 978-0-7362-7994-9

18 19   10 9

Acknowledgments and credits continue on the inside back cover.

Where is he?
Is he in the store?

No, he is in the bakery.

Where is he?
Is he in the post office?

No, he is in the grocery store.

Where is he?
Is he in the library?

No, he is in the restaurant.

Where is he now?